FLASHCARD BOOKS

CLOTHING

ENGLISH to RUSSIAN

FLASHCARD BOOK

BLACK & WHITE EDITION

HOW TO USE:

- READ THE ENGLISH WORD ON THE FIRST PAGE.

- IF YOU KNOW THE TRANSLATION SAY IT OUT LOUD.

- TURN THE PAGE AND SEE IF YOU GOT IT RIGHT.

- IF YOU GUESSED CORRECTLY, WELL DONE!
IF NOT, TRY READING THE WORD USING THE PHONETIC PRONUNCIATION GUIDE.

- NOW TRY THE NEXT PAGE.
THE MORE YOU PRACTICE THE BETTER YOU WILL GET!

BOOKS IN THIS SERIES:
ANIMALS
NUMBERS SHAPES AND COLORS
HOUSEHOLD ITEMS
CLOTHES

ALSO AVAILABLE IN OTHER LANGUAGES INCLUDING:

FRENCH, GERMAN, SPANISH, ITALIAN,

RUSSIAN, CHINESE, JAPANESE AND MORE.

WWW.FLASHCARDEBOOKS.COM

Baby Bodysuit

Детская распашонка
DEts-ka-ya ras-pa-shOn-ka

Backpack

Рюкзак

Ryuk-zAk

Baseball Cap

Бейсбольная кепка

Beis-bOl'-na-ya kEp-ka

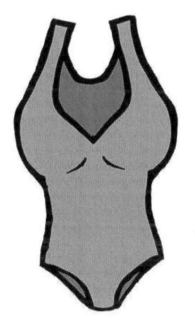

Bathing suit

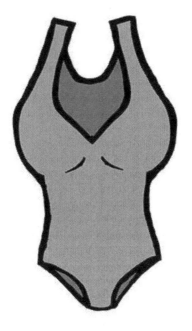

Купальник
Ku-pAl'-nik

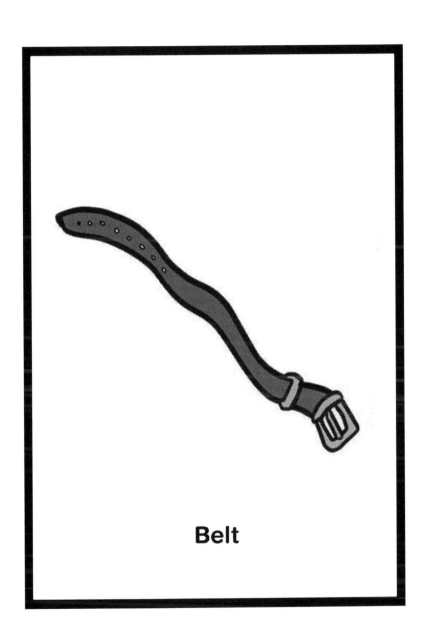

Belt

Ремень

Rye-mEn'

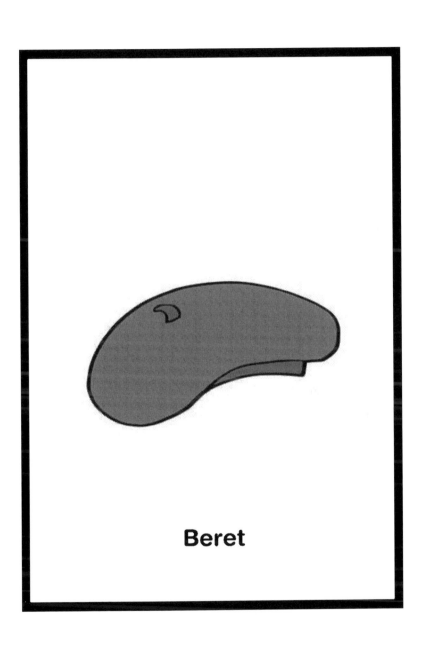

Beret

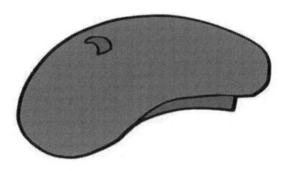

Берет

Bye-rYEt

Bib

Слюнявчик

Slyu-nYAf-chik

Boots

Ботинки

Ba-tln-ki

Bowtie

Галстук-бабочка
GAL-stuk bA-bach-ka

Boxer shorts

Боксерские трусы

Ba-ksYEr-ski-ye tru-sY

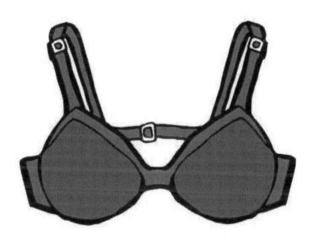

Bra

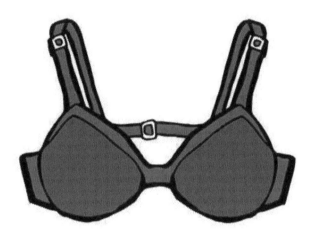

Бюстгальтер

Byust-gAl-ter

Buttons

Пуговицы
PU-ga-vi-tsy

Cardigan

Кардиган

Kar-di-gAn

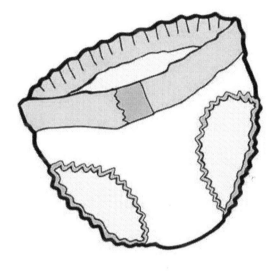

Diaper

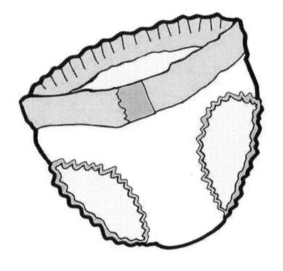

Подгузник

Pad-gUz-nik

Dress

Платье

PLA-t'ye

Dungarees

Джинсовый комбинезон
DzhIn-sa-vyi kam-bi-ne-zOn

Earrings

Серьги

SEr'-gi

Glasses

Очки

Ach-kl

Gloves

Перчатки

Per-chA-tki

Handbag

Сумка
SUm-ka

Hoodie

Кофта с капюшоном
KOf-ta s ka-pyu-shO-nom

Jeans

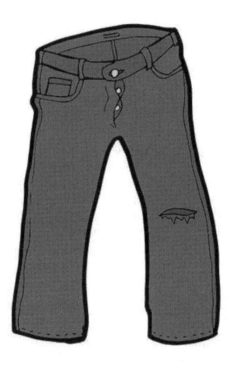

Джинсы

DzhIn-sy

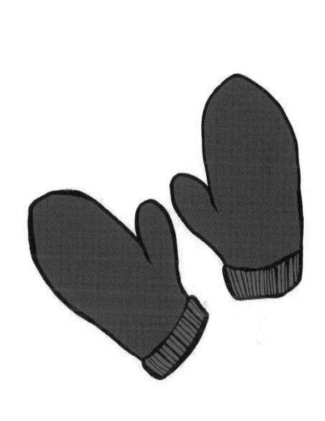

Mittens

Варежки
VA-resh-ki

Necklace

Ожерелье
A-zhe-rYe-l'ye

Pajamas

Пижама

Pi-zhA-ma

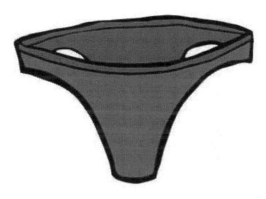

Panties

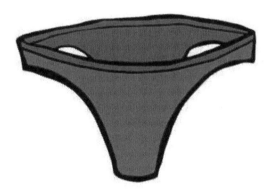

Трусики

TrU-si-ki

Party Hat

Праздничная шляпа
PrAz-nich-na-ya shLYA-pa

Rain Coat

Дождевик

Dazh-dye-vlk

Ring

Кольцо
Kal'-tsO

Robe

Халат

Ha-LAt

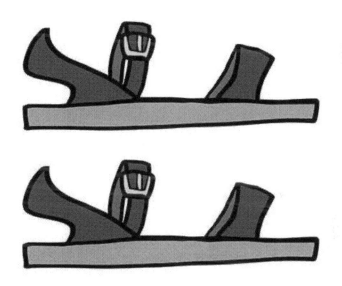

Sandals

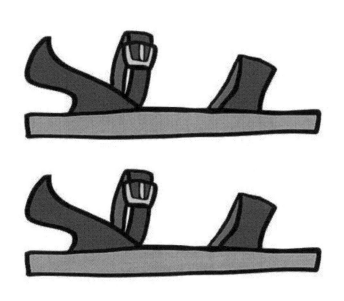

Босоножки

Ba-sa-nOsh-ki

Scarf

Шарф

Sharf

Shirt

Рубашка

Ru-bAsh-ka

Shorts

Шорты
ShOr-ty

Skirt

Юбка
YUp-ka

Slippers

Тапочки

TA-pach-ki

Socks

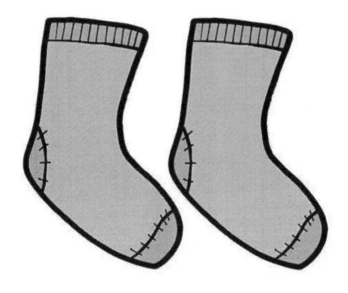

Носки

Na-skI

Suit

Костюм
Kas'-tYUm

Sunglasses

Солнцезащитные очки

Soln-tse-za-schIt-ny-e ach-kI

Sweater

Свитер

SvI-ter

Swimming Trunks

Плавки

PLAf-ki

Tee-shirt

Футболка

Fut-bOl-ka

Tie

Галстук

GAL-stuk

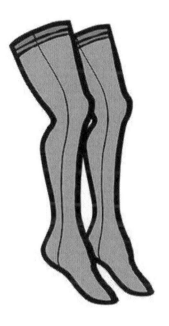

Tights

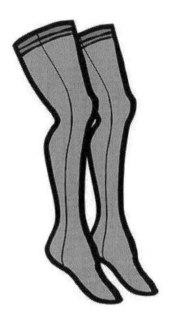

Колготки

Kal-gOt-ki

Top hat

Цилиндр

Tsi-LIndr

Sneakers

Кроссовки

Kra-sOf-ki

Trousers

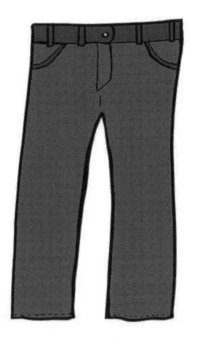

Брюки
BrYU-ki

Umbrella

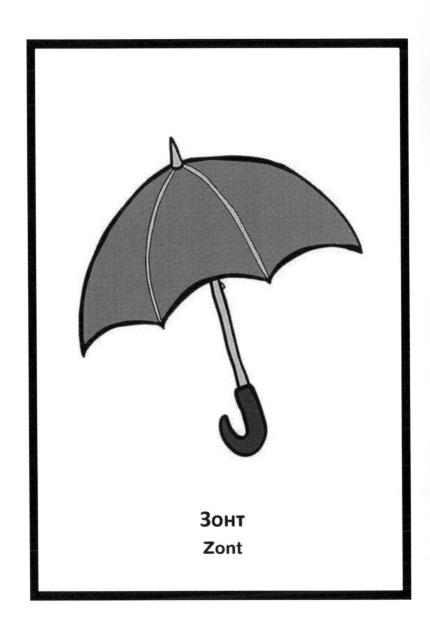

Зонт

Zont

Underpants

Трусы
Tru-sY

Vest

Майка

MAy-ka

Waistcoat

Жилетка
Zhi-LYE-tka

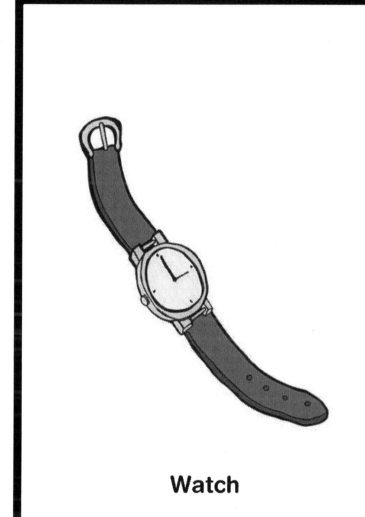

Watch

Часы

Cha-sY

Wellies

Резиновые сапоги

Re-zi-na-vy-ye sa-pa-gi

Zip

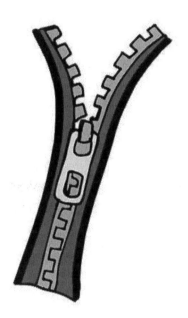

Молния

MOL-ni-ya